Charting
Made
Easy

BY JOHN J. MURPHY

About the Author

▲ ▲ ▲ ▲ ▲ ▲

John Murphy has authored three best-selling books on technical analysis, including *Intermarket Technical Analysis* and *The Visual Investor*. His latest work, *Technical Analysis of the Financial Markets* (1999), is a revised edition of his 1986 classic text which has been translated into eight languages. He is president of MURPHYMORRIS.COM which produces interactive educational products on technical analysis and online analysis for investors. As the former host of CNBC's Tech Talk show and a speaker at all the major trading and investment forums and conferences around the world, Mr. Murphy is one of the most recognized and highly respected technical analysts of our time.

This book, along with other books, is available at discounts that make it realistic to provide it as a gift to your customers, clients, and staff. For more information on these long lasting, cost effective premiums, please call us at (800) 272-2855 or you may email us at sales@traderslibrary.com.

TRADE SECRETS

Charting
Made
Easy

JOHN J. MURPHY

ISBN 1-883272-59-9

Printed in the United States of America.

Contents

Introduction

Chart analysis has become more popular than ever. One of the reasons for that is the availability of highly sophisticated, yet inexpensive, charting software. The average trader today has greater computer power than major institutions had just a couple of decades ago. Another reason for the popularity of charting is the Internet. Easy access to Internet charting has produced a great democratization of technical information. Anyone can log onto the Internet today and see a dazzling array of visual market information. Much of that information is free or available at very low cost.

Another revolutionary development for traders is the availability of *live* market data. With the increased speed of market trends in recent years, and the popularity of short-term trading methods, easy access to live market data has become an indispensable weapon in the hands of technically oriented traders. Day-traders live and die with that minute-to-minute price data. And, it goes without saying, that the ability to spot and profit from those short-term market swings is one of the strong points of chart analysis.

Sector rotation has been especially important in recent years. More than ever, it's important to be in the right sectors at the right time. During the second half of 1999, technology was the place to be and that was reflected in enormous gains in the Nasdaq market. Biotech and high-tech stocks were the clear market leaders. If you were in those groups, you did great. If you were anywhere else, you probably lost money.

During the spring of 2000, however, a sharp sell off of biotech and technology stocks pushed the Nasdaq into a steep correction and caused a sudden rotation into previously ignored sectors of the blue chip market — like drugs, financials, and basic industry stocks — as money moved out of "new economy" stocks into "old economy" stocks. While the fundamental reasons for those sudden shifts in trend weren't clear at the time, they were easily spotted on the charts by traders who had access to live market information — and knew how to chart and interpret it correctly.

That last point is especially important because having access to charts and data is only helpful if the trader knows what to do with them. And that's the purpose of this booklet. It will introduce to you the more important aspects of chart analysis. But that's only the start. The Investing Resources Guide at the end of the booklet will point you toward places where you can continue your technical studies and start taking advantage of that valuable new knowledge.

Charts can be used by themselves or in conjunction with fundamental analysis. Charts can be used to time entry and exit points by themselves or in the implementation of fundamental strategies. Charts can also be used as an alerting device to warn the trader that something may be changing in a market's underlying fundamentals. Whichever way you choose to employ them, charts can be an extremely valuable tool — if you know how to use them. This booklet is a good place to start learning how.

John J. Murphy

▲ ▲ ▲ ▲ ▲ ▲

Note from the Publisher: *Please note that trend lines, analysis, and commentary have been added to the charts for the edification of the reader.*

Charting Made Easy

Chapter 1

WHY IS CHART ANALYSIS SO IMPORTANT?

S uccessful participation in the financial markets virtually demands some mastery of chart analysis. Consider the fact that all decisions in various markets are based, in one form or another, on a market forecast. Whether the market participant is a short-term trader or long-term investor, *price forecasting* is usually the first, most important step in the decision-making process. To accomplish that task, there are two methods of forecasting available to the market analyst — the fundamental and the technical.

Fundamental analysis is based on the traditional study of supply and demand factors that cause market prices to rise or fall. In financial markets, the fundamentalist would look at such things as corporate earnings, trade deficits, and changes in the money supply. The intention of this approach is to arrive at an estimate of the intrinsic value of a market in order to determine if the market is over- or under-valued.

Technical or chart analysis, by contrast, is based on the study of the market action itself. While fundamental analysis studies the reasons or causes for prices going up or down, *technical analysis studies the effect, the price movement itself.* That's where the study of price charts comes in. Chart analysis is extremely useful in the price-forecasting process. Charting can be used by itself with no fundamental input, or in conjunction with fundamental information. Price forecasting, however, is only the first step in the decision-making process.

Market Timing

The second, and often the more difficult, step is *market timing*. For short-term traders, minor price moves can have a dramatic impact on trading performance. Therefore, the precise timing of entry and exit points is an indispensable aspect of any market commitment. To put it bluntly, *timing is everything in the stock market*. For reasons that will soon become apparent, timing is almost purely technical in nature. This being the case, it can be seen that the application of charting principles becomes absolutely essential at some point in the decision-making process. Having established its value, let's take a look at charting theory itself.

Chapter 2

WHAT IS CHART ANALYSIS?

Chart analysis (also called *technical analysis*) is the study of market action, using price charts, to forecast future price direction. *The cornerstone of the technical philosophy is the belief that all of the factors that influence market price — fundamental information, political events, natural disasters, and psychological factors — are quickly discounted in market activity.* In other words, the impact of these external factors will quickly show up in some form of price movement, either up or down. *Chart analysis, therefore, is simply a short-cut form of fundamental analysis.*

Consider the following: A rising price reflects *bullish* fundamentals, where demand exceeds supply; falling prices would mean that supply exceeds demand, identifying a *bearish* fundamental situation. These shifts in the fundamental equation cause price changes, which are readily apparent on a price chart. The chartist is quickly able to profit from these price changes without necessarily knowing the specific reasons causing them. The chartist simply reasons that rising prices are indicative of a bullish fundamental situation and that falling prices reflect bearish fundamentals.

Another advantage of chart analysis is that the market price itself is usually a leading indicator of the known fundamentals. Chart action, therefore, can alert a fundamental analyst to the fact that something important is happening beneath the surface and encourage closer market analysis.

Charts Reveal Price Trends

Markets move in trends. The major value of price charts is that they reveal the existence of market trends and greatly facilitate the study of those trends. Most of the techniques used by chartists are for the purpose of identifying significant trends, to help determine the probable extent of those trends, and to identify as early as possible when they are changing direction (See Figure 2-1).

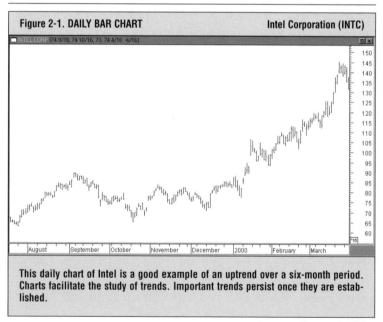

Figure 2-1. DAILY BAR CHART   **Intel Corporation (INTC)**

This daily chart of Intel is a good example of an uptrend over a six-month period. Charts facilitate the study of trends. Important trends persist once they are established.

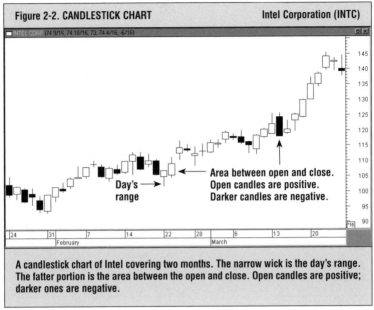

Figure 2-2. CANDLESTICK CHART   **Intel Corporation (INTC)**

Area between open and close.
Open candles are positive.
Darker candles are negative.

Day's range

A candlestick chart of Intel covering two months. The narrow wick is the day's range. The fatter portion is the area between the open and close. Open candles are positive; darker ones are negative.

Charts powered by MetaStock

Types of Charts Available

The most popular type of chart used by technical analysts is the *daily bar chart* (see Figure 2-1). Each bar represents one day of trading. Japanese candlestick charts have become popular in recent years (see Figure 2-2). *Candlestick charts* are used in the same way as bar charts, but present a more visual representation of the day's trading. *Line charts* can also be employed (see Figure 2-3). The line chart simply connects each successive day's closing prices and is the simplest form of charting.

Any Time Dimension

All of the above chart types can be employed for *any time dimension*. The daily chart, which is the most popular time period, is used to study price trends for the past year. For lon-

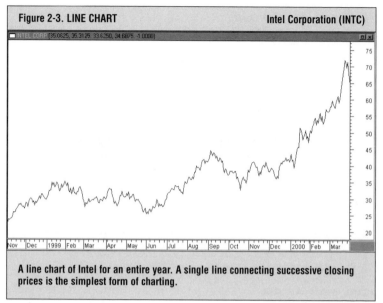

Figure 2-3. LINE CHART   **Intel Corporation (INTC)**

INTEL CORP [35.0625, 35.3125, 33.6250, 34.6875, -1.0000]

A line chart of Intel for an entire year. A single line connecting successive closing prices is the simplest form of charting.

Charts powered by MetaStock

ger range trend analysis going back five or ten years, weekly and monthly charts can be employed. For short-term (or day-trading) purposes, intraday charts are most useful. [Intraday charts can be plotted for periods as short as 1-minute, 5-minute or 15-minute time periods.]

Chapter 3

HOW TO PLOT
THE DAILY BAR CHART

P rice plotting is an extremely simple task. The daily bar chart has both a vertical and horizontal axis. The vertical axis (along the side of the chart) shows the price scale, while the horizontal axis (along the bottom of the chart) records calendar time. The first step in plotting a given day's price data is to locate the correct calendar day. This is accomplished simply by looking at the calendar dates along the bottom of the chart. Plot the high, low, and closing (settlement) prices for the market. A *vertical bar connects the high and low* (the range). The *closing price* is recorded with a horizontal tic to the right of the bar. (Chartists mark the *opening price* with a tic to the left of the bar.) Each day simply move one step to the right. *Volume* is recorded with a vertical bar along the bottom of the chart (See Figure 3-1).

Charts Are Used Primarily to Monitor Trends

Two basic premises of chart analysis are that *markets trend* and that *trends tend to persist.* Trend analysis is really what chart analysis is all about. Trends are characterized by a series of peaks and troughs. An *uptrend* is a series of rising peaks and troughs. A *downtrend* shows descending peaks and troughs. Finally, *trends* are usually classified into three categories: major,

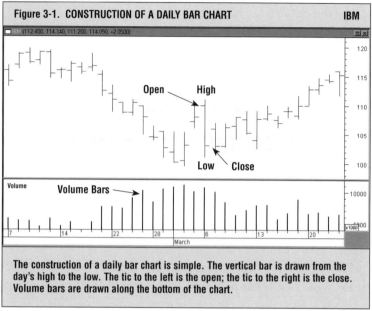

Figure 3-1. CONSTRUCTION OF A DAILY BAR CHART   **IBM**

IBM (112.400, 114.340, 111.200, 114.050, +2.0500)

Open   High

Low   Close

Volume   Volume Bars

7   14   22   28   6   13   20

March

The construction of a daily bar chart is simple. The vertical bar is drawn from the day's high to the low. The tic to the left is the open; the tic to the right is the close. Volume bars are drawn along the bottom of the chart.

Charts powered by MetaStock

secondary, and minor. A *major* trend lasts more than a year; a *secondary* trend, from one to three months; and a *minor* trend, usually a couple of weeks or less.

Chapter 4

SUPPORT AND RESISTANCE TRENDLINES AND CHANNELS

There are two terms that define the peaks and troughs on the chart. A previous trough usually forms a support level. *Support* is a level *below the market* where buying pressure exceeds selling pressure and a decline is halted. *Resistance* is marked by a previous market peak. Resistance is a level *above the market* where selling pressure exceeds buying pressure and a rally is halted (See Figure 4-1).

Support and resistance levels reverse roles once they are decisively broken. That is to say, a broken support level under the market becomes a resistance level above the market. A broken resistance level over the market functions as support below the market. The more recently the support or resistance level has been formed, the more power it exerts on subsequent market action. This is because many of the trades that helped form those support and resistance levels have not been liquidated and are more likely to influence future trading decisions (See Figure 4-2).

The trendline is perhaps the simplest and most valuable tool available to the chartist. An *up trendline* is a straight line drawn up and to the right, connecting successive rising market bottoms. The line is drawn in such a way that all of the price

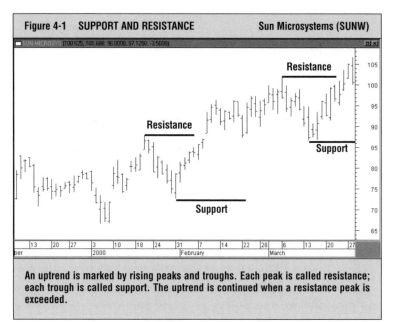

Figure 4-1 SUPPORT AND RESISTANCE   **Sun Microsystems (SUNW)**

An uptrend is marked by rising peaks and troughs. Each peak is called resistance; each trough is called support. The uptrend is continued when a resistance peak is exceeded.

Charts powered by MetaStock

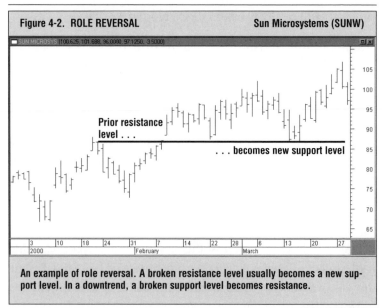

Figure 4-2. ROLE REVERSAL   **Sun Microsystems (SUNW)**

An example of role reversal. A broken resistance level usually becomes a new support level. In a downtrend, a broken support level becomes resistance.

Charts powered by MetaStock

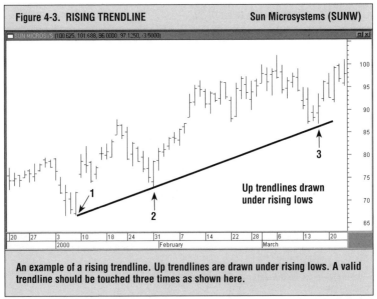

Figure 4-3. RISING TRENDLINE   **Sun Microsystems (SUNW)**

SUN MICROSYS (100.625, 101.688, 96.0000, 97.1250, -3.5000)

1

2

3

Up trendlines drawn
under rising lows

An example of a rising trendline. Up trendlines are drawn under rising lows. A valid
trendline should be touched three times as shown here.

Charts powered by MetaStock

action is above the trendline. A *down trendline* is drawn down
and to the right, connecting the successive declining market
highs. The line is drawn in such a way that all of the price
action is below the trendline. An up trendline, for example, is
drawn when at least two rising reaction lows (or troughs) are
visible. However, while it takes two points to draw a trendline,
*a third point is necessary to identify the line as a valid trend
line.* If prices in an uptrend dip back down to the trendline a
third time and bounce off it, a valid up trendline is confirmed
(See Figure 4-3).

Trendlines have two major uses. They allow identification of
support and resistance levels that can be used, while a market is
trending, to initiate new positions. As a rule, the longer a trendline has been in effect and the more times it has been tested,
the more significant it becomes. The violation of a trendline is
often the best warning of a change in trend.

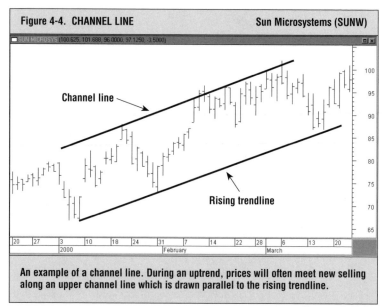

Figure 4-4. CHANNEL LINE **Sun Microsystems (SUNW)**

SUN MICROSYS (100.625, 101.688, 96.0000, 97.1250, -3.5000)

Channel line

Rising trendline

An example of a channel line. During an uptrend, prices will often meet new selling along an upper channel line which is drawn parallel to the rising trendline.

Channel lines are straight lines that are drawn parallel to basic trendlines. A rising channel line would be drawn above the price action and parallel to the basic trendline (which is below the price action). A declining channel line would be drawn below the price action and parallel to the down trendline (which is above the price action). Markets often trend within these channels. When this is the case, the chartist can use that knowledge to great advantage by knowing in advance where support and resistance are likely to function (See Figure 4-4).

Chapter 5

REVERSAL AND CONTINUATION PRICE PATTERNS

One of the more useful features of chart analysis is the presence of price patterns, which can be classified into different categories and which have predictive value. These patterns reveal the ongoing struggle between the forces of supply and demand, as seen in the relationship between the various support and resistance levels, and allow the chart reader to gauge which side is winning. Price patterns are broken down into two groups — reversal and continuation patterns. *Reversal* patterns usually indicate that a trend reversal is taking place. *Continuation* patterns usually represent temporary pauses in the existing trend. *Continuation patterns take less time to form than reversal patterns and usually result in resumption of the original trend.*

REVERSAL PATTERNS
The Head and Shoulders

The *head and shoulders* is the best known and probably the most reliable of the reversal patterns. A head and shoulders top is characterized by three prominent market peaks. The middle

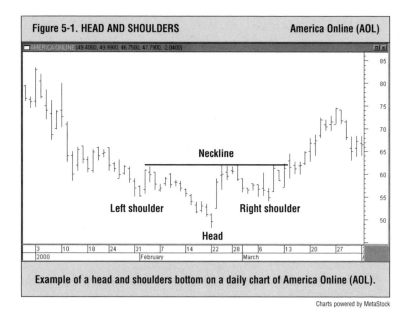

Figure 5-1. HEAD AND SHOULDERS — America Online (AOL)

AMERICA ONLINE [49.4000, 49.9900, 46.7500, 47.7900, -2.0400]

Neckline

Left shoulder   Right shoulder

Head

Example of a head and shoulders bottom on a daily chart of America Online (AOL).

peak, or the *head*, is higher than the two surrounding peaks (*the shoulders*). A trendline (*the neckline*) is drawn below the two intervening reaction lows. A close below the neckline completes the pattern and signals an important market reversal (See Figure 5-1).

Price objectives or targets can be determined by measuring the shapes of the various price patterns. The measuring technique in a topping pattern is to measure the vertical distance from the top of the head to the neckline and to project the distance downward from the point where the neckline is broken. The head and shoulders bottom is the same as the top except that it is turned upside down.

Double and Triple Tops and Bottoms

Another one of the reversal patterns, the *triple top or bottom*, is a variation of the head and shoulders. The only difference is

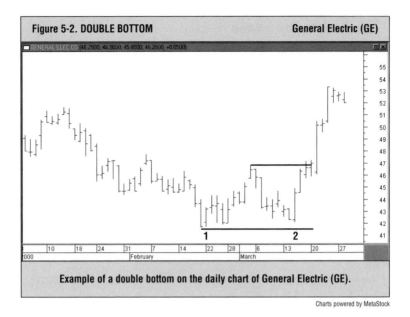

Figure 5-2. DOUBLE BOTTOM   **General Electric (GE)**

Example of a double bottom on the daily chart of General Electric (GE).

that the three peaks or troughs in this pattern occur at about the same level. *Triple* tops or bottoms and the *head and shoulders* reversal pattern are interpreted in similar fashion and mean essentially the same thing.

Double tops and bottoms (also called M's and W's because of their shape) show *two* prominent peaks or troughs instead of *three*. A *double top* is identified by two prominent peaks. The inability of the second peak to move above the first peak is the first sign of weakness. When prices then decline and move under the middle trough, the double top is completed. The measuring technique for the double top is also based on the height of the pattern. The height of the pattern is measured and projected downward from the point where the trough is broken. The double bottom is the mirror image of the top (See Figures 5-2 and 5-3).

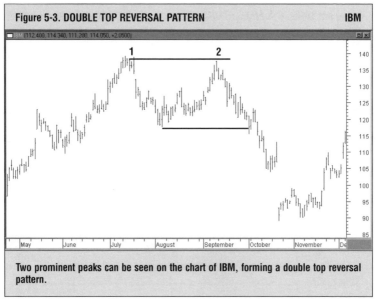

Charts powered by MetaStock

Saucers and Spikes

These two patterns aren't as common, but are seen enough to warrant discussion. The *spike* top (also called a V-reversal) pictures a sudden change in trend. What distinguishes the *spike* from the other reversal patterns is the absence of a transition period, which is sideways price action on the chart constituting topping or bottoming activity. This type of pattern marks a dramatic change in trend with little or no warning (See Figure 5-4).

The *saucer*, by contrast, reveals an unusually slow shift in trend. Most often seen at bottoms, the saucer pattern represents a slow and more gradual change in trend from down to up. The chart picture resembles a saucer or rounding bottom — hence its name (See Figure 5-5).

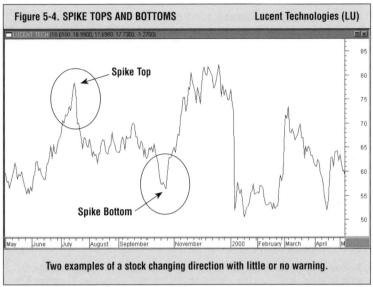

Figure 5-4. SPIKE TOPS AND BOTTOMS   Lucent Technologies (LU)

Two examples of a stock changing direction with little or no warning.

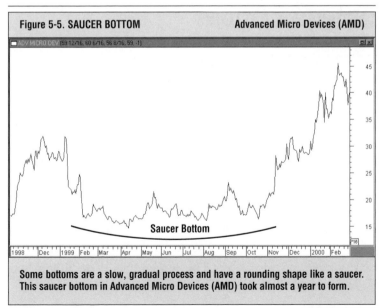

Figure 5-5. SAUCER BOTTOM   Advanced Micro Devices (AMD)

Some bottoms are a slow, gradual process and have a rounding shape like a saucer.
This saucer bottom in Advanced Micro Devices (AMD) took almost a year to form.

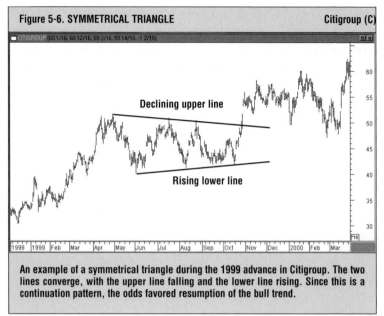

Figure 5-6. SYMMETRICAL TRIANGLE — Citigroup (C)

CITIGROUP (60 1/16, 60 12/16, 59 2/16, 59 14/16, -1 2/16)

An example of a symmetrical triangle during the 1999 advance in Citigroup. The two lines converge, with the upper line falling and the lower line rising. Since this is a continuation pattern, the odds favored resumption of the bull trend.

Charts powered by MetaStock

CONTINUATION PATTERNS

Triangles

Instead of warning of market reversals, continuation patterns are usually resolved in the direction of the original trend. Triangles are among the most reliable of the continuation patterns. There are three types of triangles that have forecasting value — symmetrical, ascending and descending triangles. Although these patterns sometimes mark price reversals, they usually just represent pauses in the prevailing trend.

The *symmetrical triangle* (also called the *coil*) is distinguished by sideways activity with prices fluctuating between two converging trendlines. The upper line is declining and the lower line is rising. Such a pattern describes a situation where buying and selling pressure are in balance. Somewhere between the halfway and the three-quarters point in the pattern, measured in calendar time from the left of the pattern to the point where the two lines meet at the right (the *apex*), the pattern should be resolved by a breakout. In other words, prices will close beyond one of the two converging trendlines (See Figure 5-6).

The *ascending triangle* has a flat upper line and a rising lower line. Since buyers are more aggressive than sellers, this is usually a bullish pattern (See Figure 5-7).

The *descending triangle* has a declining upper line and a flat lower line. Since sellers are more aggressive than buyers, this is usually a bearish pattern.

The measuring technique for all three triangles is the same. Measure the height of the triangle at the widest point to the left of the pattern and measure that vertical distance from the

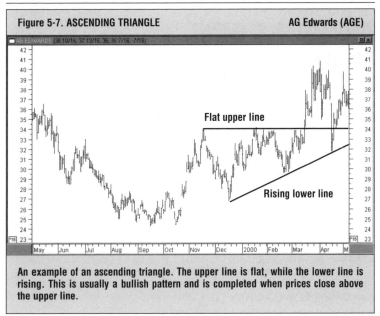

Figure 5-7. ASCENDING TRIANGLE   **AG Edwards (AGE)**

An example of an ascending triangle. The upper line is flat, while the lower line is rising. This is usually a bullish pattern and is completed when prices close above the upper line.

point where either trendline is broken. While the *ascending* and *descending* triangles have a built-in bias, the *symmetrical* triangle is inherently neutral. Since it is usually a continuation pattern, however, the symmetrical triangle does have forecasting value and implies that the prior trend will be resumed.

Flags and Pennants

These two short-term continuation patterns mark brief pauses, or resting periods, during dynamic market trends. Both are usually preceded by a steep price move (called the *pole*). In an uptrend, the steep advance pauses to catch its breath and moves sideways for two or three weeks. Then the uptrend continues on its way. The names aptly describe their appearance. The *pennant* is usually horizontal with two con-

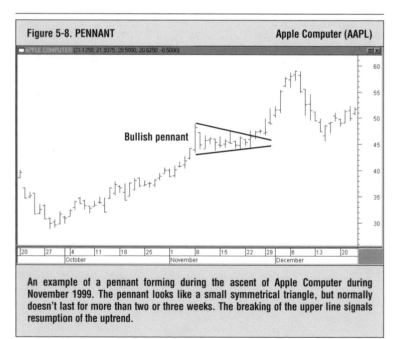

Figure 5-8. PENNANT   **Apple Computer (AAPL)**

An example of a pennant forming during the ascent of Apple Computer during November 1999. The pennant looks like a small symmetrical triangle, but normally doesn't last for more than two or three weeks. The breaking of the upper line signals resumption of the uptrend.

Charts powered by MetaStock

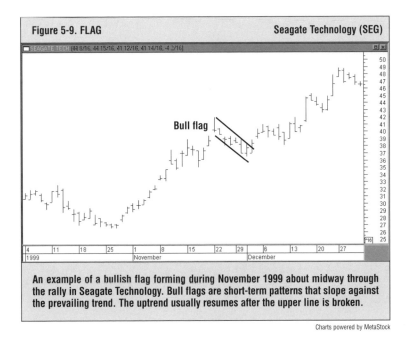

Figure 5-9. FLAG   **Seagate Technology (SEG)**

SEAGATE TECH (44 8/16, 44 15/16, 41 12/16, 41 14/16, -4 2/16)

Bull flag

4	11	18	25	1	8	15	22	29	6	13	20	27
1999				November					December			

An example of a bullish flag forming during November 1999 about midway through the rally in Seagate Technology. Bull flags are short-term patterns that slope against the prevailing trend. The uptrend usually resumes after the upper line is broken.

Charts powered by MetaStock

verging trendlines (like a small symmetrical triangle). The *flag* resembles a parallelogram that tends to slope against the trend. In an uptrend, therefore, the bull flag has a downward slope; in a downtrend, the bear flag slopes upward. Both patterns are said to "fly at half mast," meaning that they often occur near the middle of the trend, marking the halfway point in the market move (See Figures 5-8 and 5-9).

In addition to price patterns, there are several other formations that show up on the price charts and that provide the chartist with valuable insights. Among those formations are price gaps, key reversal days, and percentage retracements.

Chapter 6

PRICE GAPS

Gaps are simply areas on the bar chart where no trading has taken place. An upward gap occurs when the lowest price for one day is higher than the highest price of the preceding day. A downward gap means that the highest price for one day is lower than the lowest price of the preceding day. There are different types of gaps that appear at different stages of the trend. Being able to distinguish among them can provide useful and profitable market insights. Three types of gaps have forecasting value — breakaway, runaway and exhaustion gaps (See Figure 6-1).

The *breakaway* gap usually occurs upon completion of an important price pattern and signals a significant market move. A breakout above the neckline of a head and shoulders bottom, for example, often occurs on a breakaway gap.

The *runaway* gap usually occurs after the trend is well underway. It often appears about halfway through the move (which is why it is also called a *measuring* gap since it gives some indication of how much of the move is left.) During uptrends, the breakaway and runaway gaps usually provide support below the market on subsequent market dips; during downtrends, these two gaps act as resistance over the market on bounces.

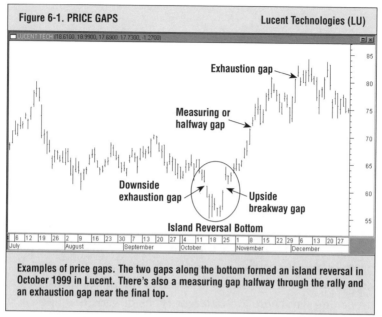

Figure 6-1. PRICE GAPS Lucent Technologies (LU)

LUCENT TECH (18.6100, 18.9900, 17.6900, 17.7300, -1.2700)

Exhaustion gap

Measuring or halfway gap

Downside exhaustion gap

Upside breakway gap

Island Reversal Bottom

Examples of price gaps. The two gaps along the bottom formed an island reversal in October 1999 in Lucent. There's also a measuring gap halfway through the rally and an exhaustion gap near the final top.

Charts powered by MetaStock

The *exhaustion* gap occurs right at the end of the market move and represents a last gasp in the trend. Sometimes an exhaustion gap is followed within a few days by a breakaway gap in the other direction, leaving several days of price action isolated by two gaps. This market phenomenon is called the *island reversal* and usually signals an important market turn.

Chapter 7

THE KEY REVERSAL DAY

A nother price formation is the *key reversal day*. This minor pattern often warns of an impending change in trend. In an uptrend, prices usually open higher, then break sharply to the downside and close below the previous day's closing price. (A bottom reversal day opens lower and closes higher.)

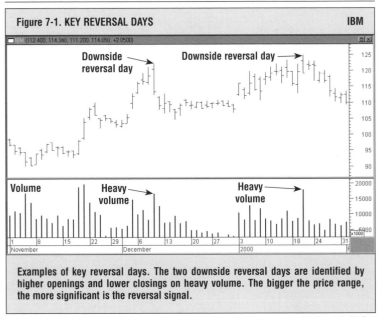

Figure 7-1. KEY REVERSAL DAYS   IBM

Examples of key reversal days. The two downside reversal days are identified by higher openings and lower closings on heavy volume. The bigger the price range, the more significant is the reversal signal.

The wider the day's range and the heavier the volume, the more significant the warning becomes and the more authority it carries. *Outside* reversal days (where the high and low of the current day's range are both wider than the previous day's range) are considered more potent. The key reversal day is a relatively minor pattern taken on its own merits, but can assume major importance if other technical factors suggest that an important change in trend is imminent (See Figure 7-1).

Chapter 8

PERCENTAGE RETRACEMENTS

Market trends seldom take place in straight lines. Most trend pictures show a series of zig-zags with several corrections against the existing trend. These corrections usually fall into certain predictable percentage parameters. The best-known example of this is the *fifty-percent retracement.* That is to say, a secondary, or intermediate, correction against a major uptrend often retraces about half of the prior uptrend before the bull trend is again resumed. Bear market bounces often recover about half of the prior downtrend.

A minimum retracement is usually about a *third* of the prior trend. The *two-thirds* point is considered the maximum retracement that is allowed if the prior trend is going to resume. A retracement beyond the two-thirds point usually warns of a trend reversal in progress. Chartists also place importance on retracements of 38% and 62% which are called Fibonacci retracements.

Chapter 9

THE INTERPRETATION
OF VOLUME

C hartists employ a two-dimensional approach to market analysis that includes a study of price and volume. Of the two, price is the more important. However, *volume* provides important secondary confirmation of the price action on the chart and often gives advance warning of an impending shift in trend (See Figure 9-1).

Volume is the number of units traded during a given time period, which is usually a day. It is the number of common stock shares traded each day in the stock market. Volume can also be monitored on a weekly basis for longer-range analysis.

When used in conjunction with the price action, volume tells us something about the strength or weakness of the current price trend. Volume measures the pressure behind a given price move. As a rule, *heavier volume (marked by larger vertical bars at the bottom of the chart) should be present in the direction of the prevailing price trend.* During an uptrend, heavier volume should be seen during rallies, with lighter volume (smaller volume bars) during downside corrections. In downtrends, the heavier volume should occur on price selloffs. Bear market bounces should take place on a lighter volume.

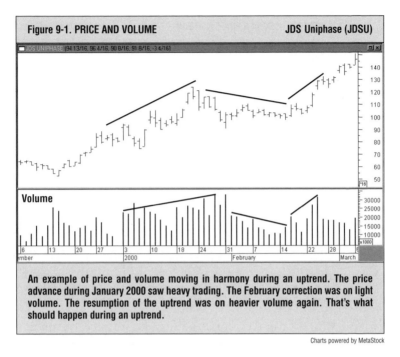

Figure 9-1. PRICE AND VOLUME   JDS Uniphase (JDSU)

JDS UNIPHASE [94 13/16, 96 4/16, 90 8/16, 91 8/16, -3 4/16]

Volume

An example of price and volume moving in harmony during an uptrend. The price advance during January 2000 saw heavy trading. The February correction was on light volume. The resumption of the uptrend was on heavier volume again. That's what should happen during an uptrend.

Charts powered by MetaStock

Volume Is an Important Part of Price Patterns

Volume also plays an important role in the formation and resolution of price patterns. Each of the price patterns described previously has its own volume pattern. As a rule, volume tends to diminish as price patterns form. The subsequent breakout that resolves the pattern takes on added significance if the price breakout is accompanied by heavier volume. Heavier volume accompanying the breaking of trendlines and support or resistance levels lends greater weight to price activity (See Figure 9-2).

On-Balance Volume (OBV)

Market analysts have several indicators to measure trading volume. One of the simplest, and most effect, is *on-balance volume* (OBV). OBV plots a running cumulative total of upside

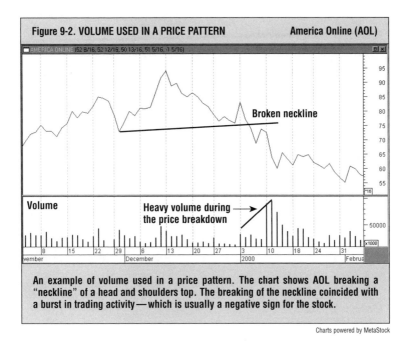

Figure 9-2. VOLUME USED IN A PRICE PATTERN   America Online (AOL)

Broken neckline

Volume

Heavy volume during the price breakdown

An example of volume used in a price pattern. The chart shows AOL breaking a "neckline" of a head and shoulders top. The breaking of the neckline coincided with a burst in trading activity—which is usually a negative sign for the stock.

Charts powered by MetaStock

versus downside volume. Each day that a market closes higher, that day's volume is added to the previous total. On each down day, the volume is subtracted from the total. Over time, the on-balance volume will start to trend upward or downward. If it trends upward, that tells the trader that there's more upside than downside volume, which is a good sign. A falling OBV line is usually a bearish sign.

Plotting OBV

The OBV line is usually plotted along the bottom of the price chart. The idea is to make sure the price line and the OBV line are trending in the same direction. If prices are rising, but the OBV line is *flat* or *falling*, that means there may not be enough volume to support higher prices. In that case, the divergence between a rising price line and a flat or falling OBV line is a negative warning (See Figure 9-3).

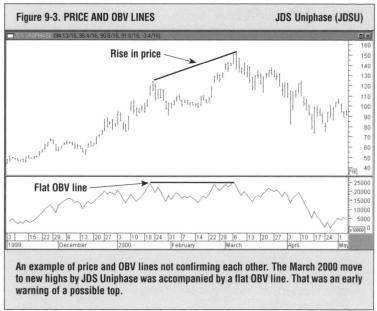

OBV Breakouts

During periods of sideways price movement, when the market trend is in doubt, *the OBV line will sometimes break out first and give an early hint of future price direction.* An *upside breakout* in the OBV line should catch the trader's eye and cause him or her to take a closer look at the market or stock in question. At market bottoms, an upside breakout in on-balance volume is sometimes an early warning of an emerging uptrend (See Figure 9-4).

Other Volume Indicators

There are many other indicators that measure the trend of volume — with names like Accumulation Distribution, Chaikin Oscillator, Market Facilitation Index, and Money Flow. While

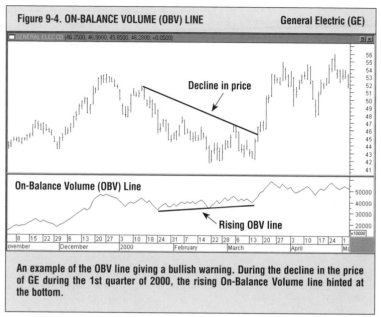

Figure 9-4. ON-BALANCE VOLUME (OBV) LINE   General Electric (GE)

GENERAL ELEC CO (46.2500, 46.3000, 45.8500, 46.2800, +0.0500)

Decline in price

On-Balance Volume (OBV) Line

Rising OBV line

An example of the OBV line giving a bullish warning. During the decline in the price of GE during the 1st quarter of 2000, the rising On-Balance Volume line hinted at the bottom.

they're more complex in their calculations, they all have the same intent — to determine if the volume trend is confirming, or diverging from, the price trend.

Chapter 10

USING DIFFERENT TIME FRAMES FOR SHORT- AND LONG-TERM VIEWS

B ar chart analysis is not limited to daily bar charts. Weekly and monthly charts provide a valuable long-term perspective on market history that cannot be obtained by using daily charts alone. The daily bar chart usually shows up to twelve months of price history for each market. *Weekly charts* show almost five years of data, while the *monthly charts* go back over 20 years (See Figure 10-1).

By studying these charts, the chartist gets a better idea of long-term trends, where historic support and resistance levels are located, and is able to obtain a clearer perspective on the more recent action revealed in the daily charts. These weekly and monthly charts lend themselves quite well to standard chart analysis described in the preceding pages. The view held by some market observers that chart analysis is useful only for short-term analysis and timing is simply not true. The principles of chart analysis can be used in any time dimension.

Using Intraday Charts

Daily and weekly charts are useful for intermediate- and long-term analysis. For short-term trading, however, *intraday charts*

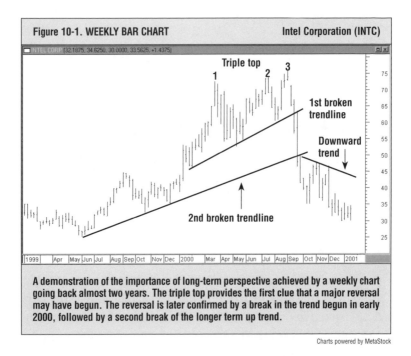

Figure 10-1. WEEKLY BAR CHART   Intel Corporation (INTC)

A demonstration of the importance of long-term perspective achieved by a weekly chart going back almost two years. The triple top provides the first clue that a major reversal may have begun. The reversal is later confirmed by a break in the trend begun in early 2000, followed by a second break of the longer term up trend.

Charts powered by MetaStock

are extremely valuable. Intraday charts usually show only a few days of trading activity. A 15-minute bar chart, for example, might show only three or four days of trading. A 1-minute or a 5-minute chart usually shows only one or two days of trading respectively, and is generally used for day-trading purposes. Fortunately, all of the chart principles described herein can also be applied to intraday charts (See Figure 10-2).

Going From the Long Term to the Short Term

As indispensable as the daily bar charts are to market timing and analysis, a thorough chart analysis should begin with the monthly and weekly charts — and in that order. The purpose of that approach is to provide the analyst with the necessary long-term view as a starting point. Once that is obtained on the 20-year monthly chart, the 5-year weekly chart should be

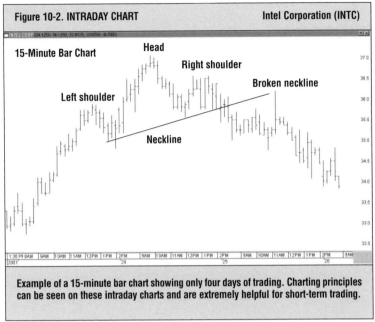

Figure 10-2. INTRADAY CHART   Intel Corporation (INTC)

15-Minute Bar Chart

Head

Right shoulder

Left shoulder

Broken neckline

Neckline

Example of a 15-minute bar chart showing only four days of trading. Charting principles can be seen on these intraday charts and are extremely helpful for short-term trading.

consulted. Only then should the daily chart be studied. In other words, the proper order to follow is to begin with a solid overview and then gradually shorten the time horizon. (For even more microscopic market analysis, the study of the daily chart can be followed by the scrutiny of intraday charts.)

Chapter 11

USING A TOP-DOWN MARKET APPROACH

The idea of beginning one's analysis with a broader view and gradually narrowing one's focus has another important application in the field of market analysis. That has to do with utilizing a "top-down" approach to analyzing the stock market. This approach utilizes a three-step approach to finding winning stocks. It starts with an overall market view to determine whether the stock market is moving up or down, and whether this is a good time to be investing in the market. It then breaks the stock market down into market sectors and industry groups to determine which parts of the stock market look the strongest. Finally, it seeks out leading stocks in those leading sectors and groups.

THE FIRST STEP: The Major Market Averages

The intent of the first step in the "top-down" approach is to determine the trend of the overall market. The presence of a bull market (a rising trend) is considered a good time to invest funds in the stock market. The presence of a bear market (a falling trend) might suggest a more cautious approach to the stock market. In the past, it was possible to look at one of several major market averages to gauge the market's trend. That was because most major averages usually trended in the same direction. That hasn't always been the case in recent history however. For that reason, it's important to have some familiarity with the major market averages, and to know what each one actually measures.

Different Averages Measure Different Things

The traditional blue chip averages — like the Dow Jones Industrial Average, the NYSE Composite Index, and the S&P 500 — generally give the best measure of the major market trend. The Nasdaq Composite Index, by contrast, is heavily influenced by technology stocks. While the Nasdaq is a good barometer of trends in the technology sector, it's less useful as a measure of the overall market trend. The Russell 2000 Index measures the performance of smaller stocks. For that reason, it's used mainly to gauge the performance of that sector of the market. The Russell is less useful as a measure of the broader market which is comprised of larger stocks.

Since most of these market averages are readily available in the financial press and on the Internet, it's usually a good idea to keep an eye on all of them. The strongest signals about market directions are given when all or most of the major market averages are trending in the same direction (See Figure 11-1).

THE SECOND STEP: Sectors and Industry Groups

The stock market is divided into *market sectors* which are subdivided further into *industry groups*. There are ten market sectors, which include Basic Materials, Consumer Cyclicals, Consumer Non-Cyclicals, Energy, Financial, Healthcare, Industrial, Technology, Telecommunications, and Utilities. Each of those sectors can have as many as a dozen or more industry groups. For example, some groups in the Technology sector

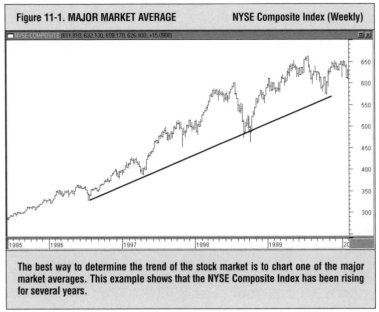

Figure 11-1. MAJOR MARKET AVERAGE   NYSE Composite Index (Weekly)

NYSE COMPOSITE (611.810, 632.130, 608.170, 626.900, +15.0900)

The best way to determine the trend of the stock market is to chart one of the major market averages. This example shows that the NYSE Composite Index has been rising for several years.

are Computers, the Internet, Networkers, Office Equipment, and Semiconductors. The Financial sector includes Banks, Insurance, and Securities Brokers.

The recommended way to approach this group is to start with the smaller number of market sectors. Look for the ones that seem to be the strongest. During most of 1999 and into the early part of 2000, for example, technology stocks represented the strongest market sector. Once you've isolated the preferred sector, you can then look for the strongest industry groups in that sector. Two leading candidates during the period of time just described were Internet and Semiconductor stocks. The idea is to be in the strongest industry groups within the strongest market sectors (See Figure 11-2).

For many investors, the search can stop there. The choice to be in a market sector or industry group can easily be imple-

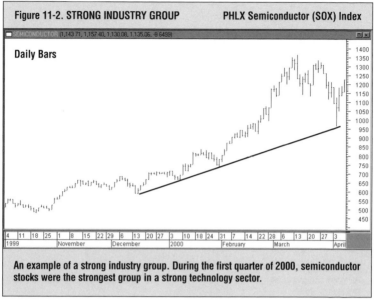

Figure 11-2. STRONG INDUSTRY GROUP   PHLX Semiconductor (SOX) Index

SEMICONDUCTOR (1,143.71, 1,157.40, 1,130.08, 1,135.06, -8.6499)

Daily Bars

An example of a strong industry group. During the first quarter of 2000, semiconductor stocks were the strongest group in a strong technology sector.

Charts powered by MetaStock

mented through the use of mutual funds that specialize in specific market sectors or industry groups.

THE THIRD STEP: Individual Stocks

For those investors who deal in individual stocks, this is the third step in the "top-down" market approach. Having isolated an industry group that has strong upside potential, the trader can then look within that group for winning stocks. It's been estimated that as much as 50% of a stock's direction is determined by the direction of its industry group. If you've already found a winning group, your work is half done.

Another advantage of limiting your stock search to winning sectors and groups is that it narrows the search considerably. There are as many as 5,000 stocks that an investor can choose from. It's pretty tough doing a market analysis of so many markets. Some

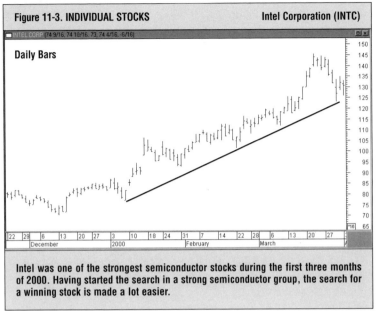

Figure 11-3. INDIVIDUAL STOCKS   **Intel Corporation (INTC)**

Intel was one of the strongest semiconductor stocks during the first three months of 2000. Having started the search in a strong semiconductor group, the search for a winning stock is made a lot easier.

Charts powered by MetaStock

sort of screening process is required. That's where the three-step process comes in. By narrowing your stock search to a small number of industry groups, the number of stocks you have to study is dramatically reduced. You also have the added comfort of knowing that each stock you look at is already part of a winning group (See Figure 11-3).

Chapter 12

MOVING AVERAGES

I n the realm of technical indicators, *moving averages* are extremely popular with market technicians and with good reason. Moving averages smooth the price action and make it easier to spot the underlying trends. Precise trend signals can be obtained from the interaction between a price and an average or between two or more averages themselves. Since the moving average is constructed by averaging several days' closing prices, however, it tends to lag behind the price action. The shorter the average (meaning the fewer days used in its calculation), the more sensitive it is to price changes and the closer it trails the price action. A longer average (with more days included in its calculation) tracks the price action from a greater distance and is less responsive to trend changes. The moving average is easily quantified and lends itself especially well to historical testing. Mainly for those reasons, it is the main-stay of most mechanical trend-following systems.

Popular Moving Averages

In stock market analysis, the most popular moving average lengths are 50 and 200 days. [On weekly charts, those daily values are converted into 10 and 40-week averages.] During an uptrend, prices should stay above the 50-day average. Minor pullbacks often bounce off that average, which acts as a support level. A decisive close beneath the 50-day average is usually one of the first signs that a stock is entering a more severe correction. In many cases, the breaking of the 50-day average signals a further decline down to the 200-day average. If a market is in a normal bull market correction, it should find new support around its 200-day average. [For short-term trading purposes, traders will employ a 20-day average to spot short-term trend changes].

Bollinger Bands

These are trading bands plotted two standard deviations above and below a 20-day moving average. When a market touches (or exceeds) one of the trading bands, the market is considered to be over-extended. Prices will often pull back to the moving average line.

Moving Average Convergence Divergence (MACD)

The MACD is a popular trading system. On your computer screen, you'll see two weighted moving averages (weighted moving averages give greater weight to the more recent price action). Trading signals are given when the two lines cross.

Chapter 13

OSCILLATORS

Oscillators are used to identify *overbought* and *oversold* market conditions. The oscillator is plotted on the bottom of the price chart and fluctuates within a horizontal band. When the oscillator line reaches the upper limit of the band, a market is said to be overbought and vulnerable to a short-term setback. When the line is at the bottom of the range, the market is oversold and probably due for a rally. The oscillator helps to measure market extremes and tells the chartist when a market advance or decline has become overextended.

Relative Strength Index (RSI)

This is one of the most popular oscillators used by technical traders. The *RSI scale* is plotted from 0 to 100 with horizontal lines drawn at the 70 and 30 levels. An RSI reading above 70 is considered to be overbought. An RSI reading below 30 is considered to be oversold. The most popular time periods for the RSI are 9 and 14 days (See Figure 13-1).

Stochastics

This oscillator is also plotted on a scale from 0 to 100. However, the upper and lower lines (marking the overbought

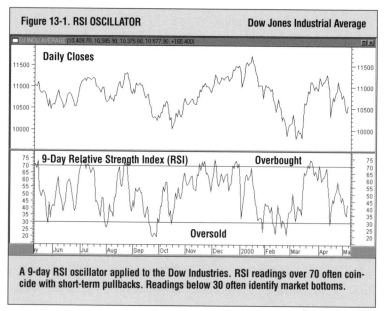

Figure 13-1. RSI OSCILLATOR   **Dow Jones Industrial Average**

DJ INDU AVERAGE [10,409.70, 10,585.90, 10,375.80, 10,577.90, +165.400]

Daily Closes

9-Day Relative Strength Index (RSI)   Overbought

Oversold

A 9-day RSI oscillator applied to the Dow Industries. RSI readings over 70 often coincide with short-term pullbacks. Readings below 30 often identify market bottoms.

Charts powered by MetaStock

and oversold levels) are at the 80 and 20 levels. In other words, readings above 80 are overbought, while readings below 20 are oversold. One added feature of stochastics is that there are two oscillator lines instead of one. (The slower line is usually a 3-day moving average of the faster line). Trading signals are given when the two lines cross. A buy signal is given when the faster line crosses above the slower line from below 20. A sell signal is given when the faster line crosses beneath the slower line from above 80. The time period used by most chart analysts is fourteen days (See Figure 13-2).

Any Time Dimension

As is the case with most technical indicators, these oscillators can be employed in *any time dimension*. That means they can be used on weekly, daily, and intraday charts. It's a good idea to use the same time span in all time dimensions. When plotting

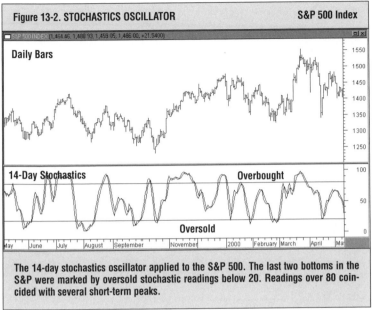

Figure 13-2. STOCHASTICS OSCILLATOR　　　　　**S&P 500 Index**

S&P 500 INDEX (1,464.46, 1,488.93, 1,459.05, 1,486.00, +21.5400)

Daily Bars

14-Day Stochastics　　　　　　　**Overbought**

Oversold

May　June　July　August　September　November　2000　February　March　April　May

The 14-day stochastics oscillator applied to the S&P 500. The last two bottoms in the S&P were marked by oversold stochastic readings below 20. Readings over 80 coincided with several short-term peaks.

Charts powered by MetaStock

the stochastics lines, for example, use 14 weeks on the weekly chart, 14 days on the daily chart, and 14 hours on an hourly chart, etc. Another reason for keeping the same numbers is that computers allow you to switch back and forth between weekly, daily, and intraday charts with a keystroke. Using the same time spans in all time dimensions makes your work a lot easier.

Chapter 14

RATIOS AND RELATIVE STRENGTH

Technical analysis can be applied to ratio charts. Trend-lines and moving averages, for example, can help measure trends on ratios and can alert the user to changes in those trends. A close monitoring of the ratio charts can add a valuable dimension to market analysis.

Sector Ratios

Chapter 11 recommended using a "top-down" market approach to find winning sectors, industry groups, and individual stocks. That is done by applying *ratio analysis* to determine each market's *relative strength*. When choosing industry groups, for example, the common technique is to divide an industry index (like the Semiconductor Index) by a market benchmark like the S&P 500. When the ratio line is rising, that means the industry is outperforming the general market. When the ratio is falling, that industry is lagging behind the rest of the market. The idea is to concentrate your attention on groups with rising ratios and avoid those groups with falling ratios. That way you'll be buying only those industry groups that are showing superior relative strength.

Stock Ratios

Once you've identified a winning group, you can apply *ratio analysis* to the stocks in that group. *Simply divide the indi-*

*vidual stocks in the group by the group index itself.*The stocks with rising ratio lines are the strongest stocks in the group.The idea here is to find the stocks in the group that are showing the greatest relative strength.That way you'll be buying the strongest stocks in the strongest groups.

Market Ratios

Ratio analysis can also be used to compare major market averages. By dividing the Nasdaq Composite Index by the S&P 500, for example, you can determine if technology stocks are leading or lagging the rest of the market.You can use the Russell 2000 versus the S&P to gauge the *relative strength* (or weakness) of smaller stocks (See Figure 14-1).

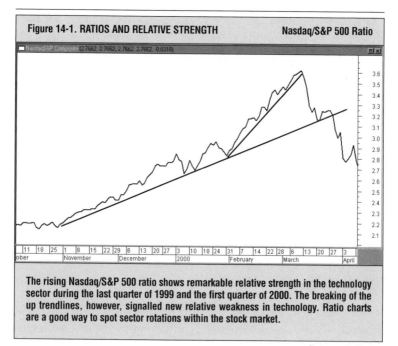

Figure 14-1. RATIOS AND RELATIVE STRENGTH   **Nasdaq/S&P 500 Ratio**

The rising Nasdaq/S&P 500 ratio shows remarkable relative strength in the technology sector during the last quarter of 1999 and the first quarter of 2000. The breaking of the up trendlines, however, signalled new relative weakness in technology. Ratio charts are a good way to spot sector rotations within the stock market.

Charts powered by MetaStock

Chapter 15

OPTIONS

Options give the holder the right, but not the obligation, to purchase (in the case of a *call*) or sell (in the case of a *put*) an underlying market entity at a specific price within a specified period of time. In its simplest application, a trader who is bullish on a market can simply purchase a *call*; a trader who is bearish can simply purchase a *put*.

The main advantage in options trading is *limited risk*. The option trader pays a *premium* to purchase the option. If the market doesn't move as expected, the option simply expires. The maximum loss the option trader can suffer is the size of the premium.

There are countless option strategies that can be utilized by option traders. However, most option strategies require a market view. In other words, the option trader must first determine whether the market price of the underlying market contract is going to rise, fall, or stay relatively flat. This is because the major factor influencing the value of an option is the performance of its underlying market. In determining an appropriate option strategy, it's important to remember that *the principles of market analysis are not applied to the option itself, but to the underlying market.*

Therefore, it can be seen that the principles of chart analysis covered in the preceding pages and their application to the financial markets play an important role in options trading.

Option Put/Call Ratio

Trading activity in the options markets is used to generate a popular stock market sentiment indicator — called the *put/call ratio*. This ratio is actually a ratio of *put* volume divided by *call* volume. It is generally applied to the S&P 100 (OEX) index option traded on the Chicago Board Options Exchange (CBOE) or the CBOE Equity put/call ratio, which uses option volume in individual stocks.

Contrary Indicator

The S&P 100 or the CBOE Equity put/call ratio is a *contrary indicator*. In other words, a high put/call ratio is considered bullish for the market (because it shows too much bearish sentiment). In the same way, a low put/call ratio (which betrays strong bullish sentiment) is considered bearish for the market. The reasoning behind the put/call ratio being used as a contrary indicator is based on the idea that option traders get too bullish near market tops and too bearish near market bottoms.

CBOE Volatility Index (VIX)

This contrary indicator is based on the volatility of the S&P 100 (OEX) index option. Since it is a contrary indicator, a rising VIX index implies greater volatility and growing concern about downside movement in the stock market. By contrast, a falling VIX implies less volatility and more confidence in the market. The VIX usually trades in a band between 30 and 20. Dips below 20 are usually associated with market peaks. Moves above 30 are usually associated with market bottoms.

Chapter 16

THE PRINCIPLE OF CONFIRMATION

The principle of confirmation holds that the more technical evidence supporting a given analysis, the stronger the conclusion becomes. In the study of an individual market, for example, all of the technical signs should be pointing in the same direction. If some signs are pointing up and the others down, be suspicious. Consult other stocks in the same group. A bullish analysis in a stock would be less than convincing if the other stocks in its group were trending lower. Since stocks in the same group tend to move together, make sure that the other stocks agree with the one being studied.

Look at the various technical indicators to see if they agree. Are the chart patterns being confirmed by the volume? Do the moving averages and oscillators confirm the chart analysis? What do the weekly and monthly charts show? While it is seldom that all of these technical factors will point in the same direction, it pays to have as many of them in your corner as possible.

Chapter 17

SUMMARY AND CONCLUSION

We have provided here an introduction to technical analysis as it is applied to the financial markets. We've discussed briefly the major tools utilized by the chartist, including: basic chart analysis, the study of volume, moving averages, oscillators, ratios, weekly, and intraday charts. The successful trader learns how to combine all these elements into one coherent theory of market analysis.

The many software and Internet-based products available on the market today also provide powerful tools that make charting and technical analysis much easier — and far more accessible to general investors — than ever before. For example, many software and Internet-based products include a full suite of technical analysis tools that allow you to create charts easily, have instant access to historical data, and have the ability to create, backtest and optimize self-designed trading systems without any programming knowledge or experience.

▲ ▲ ▲ ▲ ▲ ▲

Technical analysis provides an excellent vehicle for *market forecasting*, either with or without fundamental input. Where technical analysis becomes absolutely essential, however, is in the area of *market timing*. Market timing is purely technical in nature, so successful participation in the markets dictates some application of technical analysis.

It's not necessary to be an expert chartist to benefit from chart analysis. However, chart analysis will go a long way in keeping the trader on the right side of the market and in helping to pinpoint market entry and exit points, which are so vital to trading success. Whether the participant is a day trader or a long-term investor, it's to his or her advantage to learn about chart analysis.

Investing
Resource
Guide

▲▲▲▲▲▲

TOOLS FOR SUCCESS
IN INVESTING

SUGGESTED READING

Technical Analysis of the Financial Markets

by John Murphy

From how to read charts to understanding indicators and the crucial role of technical analysis in investing, you will not find a more thorough or up-to-date source. This comprehensive guide, revised and expanded for today's changing financial world, applies to both equities and futures markets. A must have reference, from the industry expert.

542 pp $70.00 Item #BC94x10239

Martin Ping's Introduction to Technical Analysis
A CD-Rom Seminar and Workbook

by Martin J. Ping

The foremost expert on technical analysis and forecasting financial markets gives you a one-on-one course in every aspect of technical analysis. This interactive guide explains how to evaluate trends, highs & lows, price/volume relationships, price patterns, moving averages, and momentum indicators.

The accompanying CD-ROM includes videos, animated diagrams audio clips and interactive tests. It's the user-friendly way to master technical analysis from an industry icon.

304 pp $49.95 Item #BC94x8521

▲ ▲ ▲ ▲ ▲ ▲

To order any book listed
Call 1-800-272-2855 ext. BC94

Technical Analysis Simplified

by Clif Droke

Here's a concise, easy-reading manual for learning and implementing this invaluable investment tool. The author, a well-known technician and editor of several technical analysis newsletters, distills the most essential elements of technical analysis into a brief, easy-to-read volume.

$29.95 Item #BC94x11087

How Charts Can Help You in the Stock Market

by William L. Jiler

Now a classic — this 1962 book was the first of its kind to detail specific chart reading methods to improve returns. Jiler, the president of Trendline, a division of S&P, firmly believed that anyone could improve returns with simple chart watching tactics.

$17.00 Item #BC94x2316

To order any book listed
Call 1-800-272-2855 ext. BC94

The MetaStock Difference

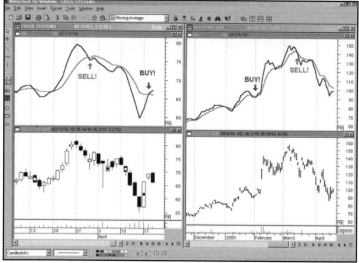

Make sure you're getting the most advanced technical analysis software available — choose MetaStock®.

Greater Depth. Study your charts with nine charting styles. Calculate moving averages with seven different methods. Plus, choose from over 120 indicators and line studies.

Create, Backtest, Optimize, and Compare Your Trading Systems. Scan your databases to find the winners. Learn from noted experts to spot important trading situations, and more. You'll never outgrow MetaStock.

Easy to Use. You only need to learn two commands to run MetaStock: Click & Pick and Drag & Drop. Moving price plots, etc. is extremely easy. And making changes to objects is even easier.

You'll Love MetaStock! MetaStock does it all. From finding what to trade, to knowing when to trade, MetaStock is available on a monthly subscription or a one-time purchase plan.

Free Data CD. Order MetaStock now and get a free data CD with over 5 years of historical data, covering over 30,000 securities.

Call for a free information pack.
1-800-272-2855
Ext. BC94

Get strong buy and sell signals with . . .

John Murphy's CPR

John Murphy's **Chart Pattern Recognition**™ (CPR), plug in software for MetaStock 7.0, can help you make better buy and sell decisions in just three easy steps!

Step 1: Find charts with good pattern trading potential. Quickly scan thousands of charts using MetaStock 7.0 from Equis and CPR. You'll find charts with definite patterns and even in the early stages of patterns.

Step 2: Focus on specific chart patterns.
With a list of the best candidates, you can now analyze individual charts with CPR and MetaStock 7.0's Expert Advisor™. CPR will label both Reversal Patterns and Continuation Patterns.

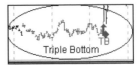
Triple Bottom

> Reversal Patterns: Head and Shoulders, Inverse Head and Shoulders, Double Tops, Triple Tops, Double Bottoms, and Triple Bottoms.
> Continuation Patterns: Symmetrical, Ascending, and Descending Triangles.

Step 3: Receive insightful, detailed commentary. Know exactly how to place your buy and sell positions, and even where to place your stops. This commentary also projects where the security price may move within a specified period of time. Also generate trading alerts with patterns. Each pattern is computer verified and supplemented with John's own expert commentary.

There is no other product on the market that implements the experience and expertise of John Murphy with the computerized technology of MetaStock. The result is simple: you'll make better trading decisions.

Call Today for your copy of CPR and MetaStock.
1-800-272-2855
Extention BC94

MetaStock®

John Murphy Products

Technical Analysis Tools from the World's Foremost Market Technician

Mastering High Probability Chart Reading Methods with John Murphy

82 min. video $99.00   Item# BC94x2044547
Renowned technical analyst John Murphy shows you step-by-step how to pinpoint the right sectors to play at the right time - with profits in tow. Citing key relationships among markets, Murphy's methods help you determine when to move from one to the other, so you're poised to capture the most lucrative opportunities available in any market climate. With a full online support manual available at www.traderslibrary.com/tradesecrets, Murphy's on-target cues for rotating among sectors will keep you in the "hot" winning ones, at the best points in the business cycle - time after time.

Intermarket Analysis: Profits From Global Market Relationships

John Murphy $69.95   Item #BC94x1523697

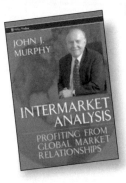

Drawing on his vast experience as both an educator and an expert trader, the author lays out his key tools to understanding global markets and illustrates how these tools can help today's serious investors profit in any economic climate. Murphy incorporates and reflects on the most recent world market data to show how seemingly disparate world markets interact and ultimately influence each other. The book includes practical applications of Murphy's popular analysis technique. Armed with the knowledge of how economic forces impact the various markets and sectors, investors and traders can profit by exploiting opportunities in markets about to rise and avoiding those poised for a fall.